I wish I could... ROAR!

A story about self-confidence

Tiziana Bendall-Brunello

Illustrated by John Bendall-Brunello

QEB Publishing

"ROAR!" said Daddy Lion, and all the little animals ran off in fright.

"Squeak!" said Little Lion.

ROAR!

Squeak!

"Don't squeak!" said Dad. "We lions ROAR!
Now go and practice roaring. Keep
practicing...ROAR...ROAR...ROAR!
I know you can do it."

Little Lion decided to practice on his mom.

"Squeak!" he called, pouncing on her.

Squeak!

"Lions don't squeak!" said Mom. "Lions ROAR!

Why don't you ask your brothers and sisters to show you how?"

"ROAR! ROAR! ROAR!
Roar! Roar! Roar!"
All Little Lion's brothers
and sisters were waking up
and roaring loudly.

ROAR!

Little Lion tried again.
"Squeak!" he said.
"Squeak! Squeak!"

squeak!

ROAR!

Roar!

Roar!

The others just laughed at him. "Lions don't squeak!" they said. "We ROAR!"

Little Lion ran away into the long grass.

"I wish I could roar," he snuffled. "But all I can do is..."

Squeak!

"Squeak!" said Mouse.

Squeak!

"Squeak!" said Little
Lion back to Mouse.

"Why are you squeaking?" asked Mouse.
"Lions are supposed to roar, not squeak!"
she said.

"Let me see if I can help you," said Mouse.

Squeak!

"It's no use," sniffled Little Lion. "I can't roar."

"Well, let's see if this helps," said Mouse.
And she whispered softly into his ear,
"ROAR! You can do it! ROAR!"

ROAR!

"Roar!" said Little Lion proudly.

"Hey!" Little Lion's brothers and sisters shouted proudly. "You've learned to roar! Hurrah! Hurrah!"

ROAR!

"We knew you could ROAR!" Daddy and Mommy
Lion said. "You just didn't know it yourself."

"Now I do!" said Little Lion triumphantly. "I can ROAR! ROAR!"

Notes for parents and teachers

- Look at the front cover of the book together. Ask the children to name the animal. Can the children guess how the animal feels?

- Can the children understand the meaning of "ROAR" and "SQUEAK"? Show them the differences between a roar and a squeak. For this exercise, focus on your posture and facial expression. Discuss how you feel when you roar and squeak, and how other people might react to these two behaviors.

- Ask the children why Little Lion cries. Discuss reasons for crying and feelings associated with crying. Do the children know the opposite of crying? At this point, it is good to discuss different types of feelings with the children (e.g. happy, sad) and associated behaviors and facial expressions.

- Ask the children why the other lions laugh at Little Lion. Is it a good thing to laugh when a friend is crying? Discuss ways in which children could help their friends when they cry.

- Can the children name all the animals in the book? Ask them which animal they like the most and why.

- Ask the children to describe what happens to the other animals when Little Lion says "ROAR." How does Little Lion look when he says "ROAR"?

- Ask the children to draw a picture of themselves saying "SQUEAK" and then saying "ROAR."

Consultant: Cecilia A. Essau
Professor of Developmental
Psychopathology
Director of the Centre for Applied
Research and Assessment in Child and
Adolescent Wellbeing, Roehampton
University, London

Editor: Jane Walker
Designer: Fiona Hajée

Copyright © QEB Publishing, Inc. 2011

Published in the United States by
QEB Publishing, Inc.
3 Wrigley, Suite A
Irvine, CA 92618

www.qed-publishing.co.uk

ISBN 978 1 60992 066 1

Printed in China

Library of Congress Cataloging-in-Publication Data

Bendall-Brunello, Tiziana.
  I Wish I Could ROAR!: A story about self-confidence / Tiziana Bendall-Brunello ; illustrated by John Bendall-Brunello.
    p. cm. -- (I wish I could--)
  Summary: Little Lion tries hard to roar like everyone else in his family but all he can do is squeak until he meets Mouse, who gives him just the encouragement he needs.
  ISBN 978-1-60992-106-4 (library bound)
  [1. Lions--Fiction. 2. Mice--Fiction. 3. Animal sounds--Fiction.] I. Bendall-Brunello, John, ill. II. Title.
  PZ7.B431352Ro 2012
  [E]--dc22
                                            2011003283